A Kaleidoscope of Paintings

Airlie Jane Kirkham

A Kaleidoscope of Paintings

Acknowledgements

'Wild Life in the City', published in *Wild*, Ginninderra Press, 2018
'Unseen memories', published in *Mountain Secrets*,
Ginninderra Press, 2019
'Morning Serenity', published in *Centre of Expression*, Noble House
Publishers, New York, 2007
'2000 and Beyond', published by poetry.com, USA, 2001
'Orchids' and 'River Sounds around the Paths', published in
FreeXpression online, April, 2019
'Bell Bird', 'Baby Magpies' and 'Lorikeets, published in *Tamba*,
Issue 64, June 2019
'Stars', published in *Poetry Matters*, Issue 37, November 2019

Thanks

Many thanks are extended to all who have helped in the production
of this book.
To my mother, who has been my amanuensis, my guiding light and
support throughout all these years.
To many friends who have read my poems and given me good
feedback: Margaret, Freda, Deb, Alison, Mary and many others.
To my mentors Rev. Dawn Colsey, Valerie Volk,
members of the group Poets of Passion.
To my mentor Jules Leigh Koch, who assisted me through the grant
project Mentoring in Poetry Writing.

A Kaleidoscope of Paintings has been assisted by a mentoring grant from,
the SA Arts Board, Richard Llewellyn Deaf and Disability Arts Trust.

A Kaleidoscope of Paintings
ISBN 978 1 76041 853 3
Copyright © Airlie Jane Kirkham 2020
Cover artwork by Pamela Margaret Kirkham
Sketches by Andrea Fidock

First published 2020 by
GINNINDERRA PRESS
PO Box 3461 Port Adelaide 5015
www.ginninderrapress.com.au

Contents

Foreword   7

The World Around
Breakout Creek – My Paradise   13
River Sounds Around the Paths   14
Haiku   15
Unseen Memories   16
Looking From My Window   18
Wild Life in the City   20
Nightfall   21
My Land   22

Birds and Creatures
Morning Lark   27
Haiku   28
Elephants   29
Charles the Turtle   30
Turtle Tales   32

Flowers
Daffodils   35
My Orchid   36
Sentinels   37
Reaching for Light   38
Haiku   39
Chrysanthemums   40
Camellias   41
Irises Ἶρις   42
Wandering Wisteria   43

Holidays
Holiday at Goolwa   47

The Bridge	48
Seaview	50
Dream Holiday	52
Wallaroo Days	54
Puffing Billy	56
Ribbon of Lifeblood	57

Adelaide

The Church View	61
ANZAC Centenary Memorial Garden Walk, Adelaide	62
Botanic Gardens in Limelight	63
The Museum	64
Adelaide Himeji Garden	65
Haiku	67

History

Discovery at the Bay	71
Holdfast Bay	73
Richard III	74
My Inheritance	75
Kith and Kin	76
Man on Mars	77

Culture

Sakura Matsuri	81
The May Queen	83
Lanterns in a Breeze	84
Monet's Garden at Giverny	86
Painting Light	88

Stitched in Memories

My Treasures	91
Collections	92
Bookmarks	93

Gifts From Abroad	94
For Sale	95
Shawls	96
Patchwork Quilt	97
Blood Tests	98

Music

Music is the Beat	103
To Music	104
The Opera House	106
My Destiny	108
Graduation Day 2.08.05	109
Master of Music	110
The Concert Hall	111
Mahler in Concert	113
Images of Music	115
Bells	116
My Heart Rejoices	118

Hopes and Aspirations

A Kaleidoscope of Dreams	121
Hope	123
New Year	124
What Love Means	125
2000 and Beyond	126
My Dream	127
Ownership	128
Peace	130
Promises	131
Musings	132
Friendly Books	134
Stars	135

Foreword

I have been writing poetry for many years. It has been a great form of rehabilitation for me, the fulfilment of a dream that I had not lost my literary skill in my accident.

Some of my earliest poems were written after I relearnt to write. Since then I have mingled with a wide range of poets, through joining the group Poets of Passion and attending poetry readings.

This collection has been developed over the last fifteen years.

I have learnt much from many people and it has helped my dream come true. There are many gems in my poetry which, I hope, will stimulate the reader to see things in the natural world differently.

My poems are paintings in a kaleidoscope of tales, themes and colours, hence the title *A Kaleidoscope of Paintings*.

As Mary Taylor from the Poet's Corner, Effective Living Centre, said to me, 'You are an artist, a painter in words.'

Airlie Jane Kirkham

The World Around

Breakout Creek – My Paradise

Soft shades of sunshine filter through tall trees
over green grassy verges beside a vibrant stream.
A creek of yesteryear
amidst old-time settlers' farmland,
now a breakout from its mother.

In solitude I walk
along its high roads and low roads
through bush with underbrush and native crimson hues.
A path well worn by feet and wheels
snakes through the blissful scene.

Willowy branches, variegated leaves,
leaning over languid water, show
rippling reflections in a shimmering, sunlit pool.
Peaceful, serene, my escape from reality.

Tall reeds entwined with gregarious grasses
are the home of the water rat.
Near stepping stones invaded by careful feet,
an egret preens itself in the mirror-like water.

The river wends its way searching for the sea
but for me this is my hidden paradise.

Breakout Creek is a local name given to a creek flowing out from the River Torrens.

River Sounds Around the Paths

Raindrops fall from trees,
leaves are trembling in the wind.
Silence is broken.

Reflections rippling,
river murmurs quietly,
startled birds fly off.

Cyclists whizz along,
crickets singing break the calm.
Is there ever silence?

Haiku

Summer nearly gone
Heavens are smiling, no rain falling
Gardens unhappy

                                  Autumn is on us
                                  Colourful leaves piling up
                                  More work for gardeners

Rivers slowing down
Wildlife has disappeared
Trees are crying leaves

                                  Acorns and gumnuts
                                  Sleeping on my garden bed
                                  Spring will awake them

Water rat peeks out
A water forager
Summer night, moonlight

Unseen Memories

Slipping from the edge of the city
I come upon the mountains,
tinged blue, misty, inviting.
I wander under a rainforest roof
like a tunnel in the mountain,
unseen by the eyes until it is chanced
upon. The path takes me along in
silent steps, in wonderment, as the
light filters through the deep gully
revealing secrets well hidden.
Fungus peeks out of undisclosed
holes.

I come upon a sparkling cascade.
Behind it, a secluded gem, a cave,
a place of shared secrets: of ancient
origins from Gondwana.
Wonders, what history, what stories
would it tell.
Droplets drip in a silver stream,
staccato like. That cascade then
creeps down the gully over rolling
stones, denuded rocks, mossy
crevices, craggy cliffs, sandstone
boulders.

I find a secret place, a pool left deep
from receding flood waters.
A bird finds its voice, a single voice
choir, a grey shrike thrush in
melodious flute-like song.
Fairy wrens join in with answering trills
a capella.
The trees whisper, the grasses dance
in the wind.
I linger, stand silently in this gully of
long dreaming.
Spellbound, I confine these gems to
my deepest dreams
before these moments slip away.

Looking From My Window

The view from my room is wonderful.
I follow the seasons,
the trees change colours and fall.
They regrow and start the cycle again.

Autumn is my favourite view,
the mellow colours of a splendid liquidambar.
Liquid gold, a name with a better effect
would be more appropriate.
Rustic hues: reds, browns,
gold and yellow.

The lorikeets come every year
to savour the tasty seeds in the catkins.
I counted twenty-eight one day.
Their colourful plumage
blended with the liquid gold.
They gave me great joy,
as I watched from my window.

Too soon the winter winds stripped the tree
of its finery, bleak and bare.
Now I could see afar to the crisp, cold city,
to the hub of life of busy people.
But it was not impressive.

Mellowness turned to coldness;
next came the vibrancy of spring.
My view was changing,
to the soft greens of spring, of new life.
Flowers adorned the gardens.
The roses brightened my view.
I thought of my new life
which I hope would begin soon, at home.

Summer is hot.
We draw the shades in my room with a view.
But I don't mind; soon that will pass
and it will return to show me
my kaleidoscope of autumn colours.
My own room which I enjoy.

Wild Life in the City

In bushland shades, the Torrens River ripples through the Linear Park.
Wild creatures claim their territory, live in their own wild world
as wardens of the river. Strange eyes peek at me
from tangled reed beds, entwined with gregarious grasses.
I see invasive insects, long-lived lacewings,
a wandering water rat, waddling water fowl
foraging hidden food or hiding under reedy bushes.
Look closely. See my companions
in a wild world at the bottom of my street.

Restless birds flit from tree to tree, full of noise and riot,
a world of freedom.
Crowds of corellas, yellow-crested cockatoos and screeching lorikeets
visit often when the liquidambar nectar feast is on.
Whoosh! In a flash they're off – this is their playground.
Leave as swiftly as they come, savour the scene
above the branches, perched on power lines.
Ducks come calling at my home, ask for breakfast,
look closely, then take flight back
to the wild world at the bottom of my street.

A pair of magpies visit my lawn almost daily.
One plunges to earth, relentlessly diving, seeking food, and then is off.
Butterflies flutter around my flower beds, never still.
At night, possums play on my roof, run in circles.
Pitter patter – murmuring loudly; by morning they are gone.
Inside my home, invisible in the murky green water of its tank,
is a reptile, a turtle flapping his flippers, seeking attention.
I wonder why we go bush. Look closely – right here, right now.
You'll find my wild world in my home, near my home
and at the bottom of my street.

Nightfall

Birds smile, sunlight fades.
Hour of sunset approaching.
Twitter dies away.

The last sunlight goes.
Slowly night creeps upon us.
Darkness is imminent.

Hope for a few stars.
Await their coming in the east.
Quiet, serene, welcome.

The sweet sleep of night.
The moon grows, stars twinkle.
The world lost in darkness.

Shadows cover views.
The moon's giant face peeps out.
Trees shiver softly.

Bats circle above
chasing the wind, never still.
The night comes alive.

Stars will fade with dawn
casting aside the nightfall.
The world awakens.

My Land

Ravaged by bushfire,
floods, sweeping rains.
The cry goes out,
'It's Climate Change!'
sceptics joining in the song.

Our land of rolling heat waves
quivers and dances
with raging rivers, fierce flying fires,
destruction and desolation.

Thirsty gardens, withered, bewildered plants,
over-ripening peaches, golden red tomatoes
on bushes burning in noonday sun
lament their predicament.

Grey clouds approach dry paddocks,
waiting the fall of steady, soaking rains,
like sounds of muffled drums,
bringing liquid gold.

Brown streams inching their way, now
creep subtly into homes perched precariously
beside creek beds burnt dry.
The rain goes – choruses of crickets arise
from well-hidden places in soggy gardens.

But has the climate really changed in
a land ravaged by multiple fires,
floods, droughts and famine
ever since the first settlers arrived?

I love this land, our home.
Weather vagaries are part of its being
despite scepticism, heartbreaking at times.
But our land rises in great splendour
above adversity.

Birds and Creatures

Morning Lark

Morning lark, that's me.
I love to wake early.
You will hear me singing
any time after three.

I stay awake all day,
I've lots to do, keep busy,
but later in the afternoon
I have a rest at three.

At night I fall asleep
in front of the TV,
but early in the morning,
I come alive at three.

Haiku

A bellbird calling
Echoing over the river
No one answers

                                     Baby magpies
                                     Share voices with mynahs
                                     Not indifferent

Lorikeets screeching
Pecking tree fruits and flowers
Well fed, no voice left

                                     Dragonflies skimming
                                     Moving along to music
                                     Over the water

Sounds move upon the waters
bees humming, murmuring
Single melody

Elephants

On the level plain of my buffet,
silently several elephants parade
like unhurried turtles.
Elephant-coloured, still.

Small, black, some without a tusk or two,
like bees without a sting.
Sleek, once shiny, mute monsters,
their great hulks reduced to minis.

Seedy, searching, beady eyes,
artificial, no trumpeting,
coolly watching. Unforgetful.
A menagerie perhaps.

Intricately carved, two large brown
elephants stand guard,
like mother and father,
somewhat faded, like Chinese jade.

Pondering the situation, observant.
What stories they could tell
of life in my jungle.

Charles the Turtle

Deep green water,
murky and still.
Pebbles and stones.
Where is Charles?

He's curiously gazing
through the glass.
Hark! Does he hear
the freezer door?

He's always hungry
for tasty morsels
like frozen fish,
nibbles of turtle food.

Patience is not his style.
He flaps his flippers
like a bird taking off.
He nearly does when the freezer opens
with an icy crackle.

At times he is pensive,
staring through the gloom
of murky uncleaned water.
Stones scattered singly along the tank floor.

But he's fun when he looks dolefully
into the eyes of his mistress –
Jumps to attention
on his back legs
anticipating a tidbit.

Ah well! He's disappointed again.
It's not teatime yet.

Turtle Tales

One wonders how he communicates.
Friendly creature, wags his flippers,
clever, senses every movement
in his room, demanding
morsels, tidbits, food,
especially when the fridge door is opened.

Sociable, always ready to snap a few fingers.
Creates chaos in tank.
Loves chewing tiny toys, climbing on pontoon,
basking in morning sunlight
filtering through shaded windows.

A demolition dozer,
pulls apart plants and fake flowers
displayed elegantly in his tank.
Climbing up wall, ready to jump out.
He did one day.

Exercises vigorously every day,
swimming and diving around the wide tank.
Creates his own music band
from striking sounding stones
padding on the floor.

A creature of mystery and amazement.
That's my talented turtle.

Flowers

Daffodils

It's Daffodil Day,
passionate, caring, thoughtful,
many people helping.

Bright yellow new life,
loving, responding, giving,
provides many cures.

Happy daffodils
growing, flowering, spreading.
People are smiling.

My Orchid

One day, surprising,
my friend arriving
with orchid in hand.

Two heads of flowers,
in brilliance and hue,
standing erect and

proud of itself; tall
like a sentinel.
Home-grown with water,

with care and concern,
with shades of purple
like colourful flags –

petals touch'd with white.
Dining on water,
living in sunlight

like lazy flowers
doing nothing but
seeking admirers.

Sentinels

Standing slim and tall,
fine orchids, everlasting,
sentinels at large.

Tinted flowers bloom.
Do they know how great they are?
Touched with perfume.

A delight for all,
chosen well by my good friend.
Admired every day.

Reaching for Light

Brilliant purple hue
Stand erect, fresh, long-lasting
Heads held high, heavenly.

Natives? Not home grown
Buds on stem reaching for light
Imported perhaps.

Carefully picked
Tropical purples display
Cream and pink edges.

Haiku

Red flowering gum
Watches sunset with rich colours
Quietly praising

Chrysanthemums

Unseen for months, they emerge,
bustling into shops with predictable precision.
Found, too, lining the highways,
graveyards, at cemetery gates,
in boxes, sitting proudly on firm stalks.

The doorbell rings heralding the arrival of
an itinerant local woman
with clutches of saleable flowers:
'Won't you buy my pretty flowers,' she sings.

Mother's Day welcomes multicoloured chrysanthemums
displayed in buckets, bouquets, bunches,
potted, singles or doubles, parading curled or frilled petals.
Then golden glory, with perfectly moulded heads,
each massed in colourful loveliness.

White for the purity of a mother's loving care,
purple and lilac for compassionate devotion,
yellow, burnished brown pompons,
for joy and celebration.

Memories of mothers, grandmothers
flood the scene, as if looking down in eternal love.
Too soon the chryssies will be gone for another year.

Camellias

Coloured white, speckled pink,
Striped, double, crossbred.
Dad named it 'Airlie'; my favourite flower,
nurtured from a self-sown seed
over seven long years.

Amidst its companions,
it stands guard along the south.
Many other varieties have
lived well in our garden.

Summer ravaged the camellias.
Liking a cool climate,
the bushes wilted, deprived of water,
despite hand-held buckets
cascading washing machine relics.

Branches became stark,
denuded of leaves, fallen
like a carpet below.
It brought tears to my eyes.

Winter rains have replenished the soil.
New growth is imminent,
encouraging bulging buds on branches.
Will my camellias survive another summer?
Will our backs survive another round of carting water?

Irises Ἶρις

Within the tangle of bulbs and roses
stands my rainbow.
Derived from the Greek for peace
five lights in an unveiled garden
please me in their quiet beauty.

Dutch irises, blooming suddenly
with a burst of spring weather,
though shy, hold their heads erect,
upright and true. Not blue,
but purple, they brighten my spirit.

Pendant petals, opening downwards,
fall, distinctive along their spines.
They grace my garden, my special sight.
Rainbows, painted white and yellow,
surrounded by deep purple.

My dream of a rainbow rises over the sky.
Soon their colour will fade away,
disappear, all but forgotten,
until spring offerings again become their heirs.

Iris (Ἶρις)

Wandering Wisteria

From my window,
a long curtain of flowers,
a veil of short-lived lilac lace
grows vigorously around the pergola.

A small plant at first,
newly placed in welcoming patio ground.
Shoots spread out,
clinging tenuously to the wood,
trunk and limbs unknowingly
reaching for the sky.

Soon, swaying in the breeze
like sails flapping at sea,
holds on like an anchor,
almost strangling its support.

Each winter's prune devastates its well-being.
Regrows exuberantly,
the pergola bows under its weight.
Despondent, reduced to rotten wood;
it too, bows, bends, and finally gives in.

Wisteria, clad in brilliance stands tall.
No need for pergola.
Wisteria groans, not foreseeing its ruin.
Only one trunk to stand alone.

Each year, a new burst of growth.
Tender tendrils emblazoned with purple,
grasping, covering, strangling
unaware of its future.

Holidays

Holiday at Goolwa

Our time is our own,
we can do as we please,
our hopes are on high
as we walk in the breeze.

Home away from home,
we can sit in the sun,
or walk on the beach
while we have lots of fun.

Goolwa, my holiday place,
a home by the sea,
with lakes and islands
as far as the eye can see.

We come here to rest.
We find peace and much calm.
I love to see new sights
while in places of balm.

We ride on the ferry,
We drive in the car,
We look at the wildlife
from near and afar.

Now good times must end
but return we shall do.
We love the serenity,
for me and for you.

The Bridge

Goolwa, Hindmarsh Island Bridge

A single span,
standing high,
silver, sleek.
Murals on side
highlighting the controversy.

Is it wanted?
Loved, or despised?
Too many have stood at its foot
wavering, agreeing,
dissenting.

Like a bird with one wing,
it stretches out
to touch the island.
Is serenity lost forever?
Peace, islanders' retreat?

Or will the vehicles, boats
and the like,
bring prosperity and fame?
Time will tell.

Issues alive now
will fade with the sunset
over this haven for birds.
People, intruders,
will come and go.

The water flows quietly to the sea.
The birds wheel, call,
oblivious to the uproar,
of waves, of people.
After all, they were there
with the original owners
of this land.

We respect the bridge;
the Aboriginal heritage.
Can both live together
in harmony, as one,
in this land of lakes and islands?

Seaview

A view along the shore amid
the sea and cabins.
Magnificent long beach,
seaweed hills, uncovered sandbars,
distant tide – where is the shoreline?

Hidden beneath the sand,
blue crawlers brighten the shimmering pools,
a tasty meal,
if one can catch them.

The boardwalk is lengthy.
I take a ride along its
full dimensions.
Meet a cliff.
I'll give that a miss.
Farewell to its mightiness.

I long to feel the sand but it's
out of reach.
I'll try something else.
Did I see snorkellers,
canoeists, swimmers
treading water in a recreational bay?

Norfolk pines gird the wayside.
Paths, neatly clad
in designer pavers,
sweep around the fringes of a pristine bay.

No fish, no crabs
no shells. Only sea-grass
litters the sands lying
in glassy poolets
mirroring the sky,
left bare in the wake of retreating waters.

Cosy cabins with all necessities,
home away from home.
Wistful relaxation and windy seascapes
interspersed with sweet sunshine
and time to reflect.

Dream Holiday

I dream of my holiday,
a butterfly flying away,
flight of fancy, to distant places:
cruise to New Zealand, my latest whim.

To Sydney, where the *Dawn Princess*,
a huge ship, rises majestically from the sea.
New places, exotic climes,
long days at sea – not a millpond –
lead us to our destination.

Birds abound. Little scenery
except those three mighty islands,
Kings on distant horizons.
Visiting tourist delights are in my dreams.
The butterfly settles on each one momentarily,
then off and away.

Bay of Islands with its scintillating waters,
steeped in history.
My eye in my mind spies the mighty flagpole,
views the rocks and archways over raging seas.
The Maoris in a historic treaty house
are more peaceful than yesteryear.

Harbours and islands,
volcanic lakes and eruptions.
Bubbling mud pools
or crystalline terraces
glimmering in rustic colours in the sun.

My flight of fancy takes me south,
viewing the capitol, with its Beehive,
whales basking in the sunny, warm seas.
visit the quaintly coloured village Akaroa
with its French street names.

The ship glides effortlessly to
the quietness of havens and fiords.
The Mitre Peak stands like a colossus
overpowering sea waters below.

Hikers tramp their weary way
to hostel rest.
But we survey the scene from comforting heights
and trendy deckchairs.

My mind takes flight, like a butterfly,
reminiscences from my mind's memory.
My mind may be shut in a diving bell
but it is still like a butterfly, fancy-free.

Inspired by the book *The Diving Bell and the Butterfly* – Jean-Dominique Bauby

Wallaroo Days

Departure

We left for a world unknown.
Long drive, roads renowned for variations,
sometimes as smooth as a silk cushion,
but impregnated with black patches
nonchalantly scattered to provide bumps,
excitement, my hair tossing in the swaying van.

Arrival

Each day is a moment with purpose: we cherish each one.
Our first view of a magnificent seashore.
The wind in my sails, I drive along
overlooking an expanse of low-tide debris
and dunes of stunted bush. The evening's beauty as if
a postcard picture of the sunset.
Sweet dreams.

Day 2

A quiet town, with interesting history,
Seafaring, mining, relics from Cornwall,
made modern with pristine paving and modernity,
indulging in buildings old and new.
Museum archives old keepsakes for tomorrow,
while coffee houses dwell in
old, long-forgotten bond houses
and taverns for sailors.

Day 3

An enormous jetty
reaching from derelict copper mining remains
to almost the horizon.
A ship quietly loads grain.
Fishermen scattered along a slated edge are laidback.
Occasional crabs which found themselves captured
in a net are randomly thrown back to the sea.

Day 4

Heritage is nearby, carved in sandstone.
The influence of settlers of 150 years ago,
is felt, fascinatingly casting a dominating shadow
over Victorian relics – beauty to behold.
Cousin Jack and cousin Jenny
remind us of our Cornish forebears.

Day 5

The little train of toylike dimensions
rattles around the lost years of the mine
redolent of the search for copper, a new life
from immigrants brought to this valuable land.
The old engine house, shafts, and banked up tailings
with walls built of copper-streaked rocks, are
a grim reminder of century-old times of prosperity.

Departure

As we leave, we have a lingering look.
Yes. We will be back again.

Puffing Billy

A train with a name, Puffing Billy,
Smoke, steam,
ferny glades.
Bridges up high, hang out for a view.
Wattle trees, English elms
add lustre to bushy land.

Wayside stops.
Emerald, glowing in the rain.
Lakeside, destinations of many.
Toot, toot, return journey.
The guard with his green flag
urges us on.

Relax. The bush in reverse
is inviting.
Bushwalkers tracing the route
alongside the track.
We descend. A quicker journey.
The time is well spent
on Puffing Billy.

Ribbon of Lifeblood

The time of drought has gone.
No more talk of a river dying.
Its thick waters are back,
with birds wheeling overhead, following
the wake, flinging wild water into the air.
The Murray is in my sights.
Cruising, whatever way, my delight.
I did it! My chair afloat,
unbelievable, on a dry deck.

Natural wonders on port and starboard.
The tatters of old bark, bent and ugly,
overlooking the edge of the swampy verges.
Edging along, there are fleeting glimpses
of a water creature displaying itself
indiscriminately and unguarded.

What wonders are lying latent in the muddy banks?
A fish leaps, unexpectedly,
unaware of birds who dive,
while a tern takes his fill
and tries again for more.

Changing course avoids river sand bars,
and houseboats, encroaching on our route,
are like beetles afar off, invading our territory.
Jet-skiers scream past us like engines in full bore.

The river moves with its own purpose,
reminiscent of paddle steamers
winding their way along this ribbon of lifeblood,
a tireless stream oblivious of those
who ride its back today.

Adelaide

The Church View

The shades outside keep off the sun,
redolent of that first service
under a ship's sail
brought from the port in 1836.

Inside we contemplate the memory
of the early pioneers display
on white wall plaques.
The scene is set for us.

The organ reverberates with magnificent tones
commanding the chancel
as the golden eagle looks sternly from the lectern
at the carved wooden pews.

The great leadlight, stained glass window
in translucent colours depicts St Paul and the apostles
praising the risen Christ seated on his heavenly throne.
The archway states the beauty of the earth in its holiness.

But time has brought change –
different cultures now meet inside,
and under the sails outsides, Mandarin mingles in conversations
with Australian, English, or African dialects,
while children run boisterously across the grass.

Holy Trinity City Church, North Terrace, Adelaide

ANZAC Centenary Memorial Garden Walk, Adelaide

A walk of courage
emulating every step, each footstep taken
in service for our country.
We remember those who, undaunted,
made the supreme sacrifice for our freedom.
Now in lonely graves on classic ground.

The memorial stands proudly at the entrance.
The walk to Gallipoli is redolent
of yesteryear, as the Diggers
clambered up those steep, craggy cliffs
in desperate hours.
Heroic exploits, an immortal charge
undeterred by threat of miscalculated danger.

A walk of courage, dignity,
humility and determination.
A pathway of honour, of valour, of endurance.
Three pillars of symbolism –
remembrance, service, loyalty.
They are now at rest, deserving honour.
A walk which carves the ANZAC name in history.

Botanic Gardens in Limelight

The Italian garden:
a courtyard in a secluded spot,
fountains and ponds.
Sculptures rest elegantly
on pedestals, amid leafy alcoves.
Purple and gold, rich Roman hues
abound in this quiet place.
Gardens in their prime,
flowers bloom, wisteria in bowers,
winding pathways,
a trail of nature in abundance.

Roses in a whirl circle the lawns.
Red, mauve, yellow, white, arches of colour.
Each one nurtured, its petals ablaze,
fragrant and aromatic.

The crystal shape of the palm house
like a jewel newly restored,
is a sparkling backdrop.

I love walking in the garden,
beside lakes with ducks,
birds and swans, age-old trees and palms.

The myriad species,
hues, shapes, and sizes.
A masterful scene.
Most of all,
there is peace and serenity.

The Museum
North Terrace, Adelaide

Animals in glass cases,
birds swooping from ceilings,
skeletons out of cupboards.

Egyptian mummies
wondering where their daddies are,
vases and coins, glass-coloured jars.

Insects and other things,
just a bit stuffed,
and mounted on walls,
colourful, distinct.

Vast halls full of natural wonders.
We peer and peek,
love to play hide and seek
in dark corners,
overshadowed by elephants,
whales and dinosaurs.

Bones, dry and brittle,
glued together to make
shapes, to deceive us
into thinking it's prehistoric.

Artefacts, souvenirs.
A museum full of heritage,
history, happenings,
from this wonder world
in which we live.

Adelaide Himeji Garden

South Terrace, Adelaide

In hidden shades,
a garden of imagination
dwells,
away from the life of the bustling city.

Its charm bestows
remembrance of its motherland,
a place of contemplation.
A water bowl – *chozubacchi* – to purify oneself,
adopt a humble attitude
to appreciate the grandeur of nature.

The lantern of friendship – *okunoin doro*
and the lake – *s'ensui* – based on – *shin* –
the heart or soul of this wondrous place:
calm water leads to life.

Feel the tranquillity bringing
purity and peace to the heart,
achieving happiness.
Natural elements symbolise
great features of nature, a waterfall
redolent of wild mountain torrents.

The tea house – *chashitsu* – overlooks
the sea of sand.
How I long for wisdom,
serenity and calm.
Those perfectly raked pebbles,
white and sparkling, evoke
a world of vastness and seas.

The mountains – *tsukiyama* –
in the centre of the universe –
the harmony of Yin and Yang –
balance the lowliness of the lake.
A garden of profound religious significance.

Sage green hues, bushes,
dark black pine trees – *matsu* –
symbolise courage and immortality.
Follow the *tobiishi* – stepping stones –
walking slowly in admiration

Haiku

Himeji Garden
Bushes aflame with colour
Autumn expression

White pebbles glisten
Sit quietly to meditate
Solace in my mind.

History

Discovery at the Bay

A visit of discovery highlighted my day –
the ship *Africaine*, redolent of that first day,
sailing proudly after a long and arduous journey
to a new land, by Kangaroo Island, Cape Jervis,
Rapid Bay, into a bay to hold fast to life.

Remember those early settlers, thankful,
full of hope, ambition, cherishing every moment.
Imagine those eager faces watching their arrival from the deck,
looking over with a sense of wonder
where they would land next, and stay.

A new life awaits, expectations unknown –
a tent home, a mud house, a wooden hut?
Seeing the unforgettable, the reality,
the intimidating but awesome beauty of this land.

Recall the fortitude of women and children,
encouraged earlier by Light, Kingston and Gouger,
suffering oppressive heat, hardships,
the cruel perseverance of flies,
and malevolent, malicious mozzies.

Heed the arrival of the *Buffalo*
sometime later, bearing powerful men
proclaiming ownership of this new land,
ready to design a new settlement.

The raising of the flag amidst gum trees
near the bay bearing the new name – HOLDFAST –
Hindmarsh encouraging celebration and proclamation.

Each moment evokes a spell, a purpose.
The reason for the long journey is revealed.
The *Africaine* slips quietly away.

The *Africaine* left Southampton on 2 July 1836, arrived Kangaroo Island 4 November 1836, Rapid Bay 7 November 1836, Holdfast Bay 17 November 1836. The *Buffalo* arrived at Holdfast Bay on 28 December 1836. (The Bay Discovery Centre, Glenelg)

Holdfast Bay

A dusty land, native trees,
untouched sandy shore
greeted those pioneers who landed
in Holdfast Bay long ago.
I stand in awe of them.
What did they think of their new home, the Bay?

Recall their fortitude as powerful men
proclaimed ownership of this new land.
Hardship, flies, lack of food,
sunburn, malicious mozzies, all no more.
What would they now think of the Bay?

>Pristine sands, high-rise hotels, no more mud houses,
>the dusty lanes replaced by tram tracks.
>Ice cream parlours, coffee and cake shops,
>nice chocolate nooks, and bustling boutiques.
>Would they have foreseen such a futuristic Bay?

No expectation of such a forlorn place
becoming a civic community, of holiday makers,
revellers, commercialisation, shopping till you drop.
The awesome beauty of their environment,
their once new life at the Bay gone forever,
but always remembered.
Would they be happy or sad with the Bay of today?

Richard III

A tribute to his reburial in Leicester Cathedral, 2015

Cannons in salute,
redolent of the battlefield
530 long years ago.

After death, stripped naked,
strung ignominiously across a horse.
White rose crown lost, wrenched from his skull,
found on a Bosworth thornbush.
Red rose crown now adorning Henry Tudor.

Cold bones, buried without ceremony,
incognito in a friary, found under an old concrete car park.
Child of a protagonist,
Fotheringhay, Middleham, London now forgotten.

Long shadows cast over glimpses of a king,
once lost long, now in light forever found.
Laid to rest with prayers
for courage, forgiveness and humility.

Well deserving dignity and honour,
Richard's name carved again in history.
a transforming legacy of the last Plantagenet king.

My Inheritance

My nanna left me a new home
for my books, a wonderful piece of furniture
designed and turned by my poppa.

The carved spiral legs are eye-catching,
unique, antique and sculptured
in Charles II or Queen Anne style,
more likely William and Mary.

Its glass door is resplendent
and transparent, for all to view
my most valued books.

Unique, antique and sculptured,
the envy of all who come,
it stands tall and proud
against the wall,
admired by everyone.

Kith and Kin

A long mystery, finding my forebears.
Search and tramp the countryside,
finding my roots, branches,
many other trees, intertwined.

Fascinating history.
A new discovery delights.
Another cousin, is it second or ninth,
or too distant a number?

Searching indices, wills, books,
Googling at a web. What will turn up next?
A photo of great great grandmother?
An ancient churchyard tomb?

How many Williams in my family?
Who is John? Is Mary his wife or Sarah?
Where did Joseph live? Essex or Cornwall,
Scotland or Geordieland,
Yorkshire or Cumberland,
all beckon me.

An expanding jigsaw,
piecing together bit by bit.
Where do they belong?
A mystery to unravel.
But it's fun.
Might I be connected to royalty?

Man on Mars

Man on the moon again,
or will it be Mars?
Again – that giant step for mankind,
to seek lands at the end of time?

I was only four
when that first step was made.
So I wonder why
it was not repeated sooner.

Man is not immortal;
those steps are few and far
as he reaches out
beyond his destiny.

A planet or moon, full of dead things,
rocks, no life, barren and waterless.
Why is man so keen?
Can life as we know it survive?

Red, boulder-strewn.
The eagle has landed.
Great exhilaration.
What next? A boost for man.

Like explorers of old,
people are not content
until they see what is
on the other side of the world.
Or the universe.

Thirty-nine years later we see again
that giant stride for man.
Now he knows no bounds.

We are left wondering
who will be so bold to live on Mars,
to seek lands at the end of time?

Culture

Sakura Matsuri

Cherry blossom, Japan's national flower

Glowing pink,
Sakura, seen, worshipped
by all true Japanese.
Hanami – flower viewing.
The festival is divine.
The new blossom from the gods
heralds the first signs of spring.

All celebrate with fine food, sake,
kirin beer, delicacies, Japanese pancakes,
noodles and yakitori.

Picnic rugs, blue tarpaulins
under the blooms.
Stake your claim,
celebrate a festival.

Matsuri is evident.
Shakuhachi sounds fill the air,
the beat of the taiko.
whole families resplendent in kimonos.

The gardens are dressed in *sakura*
everywhere on hillsides,
along canals, rivers, parks.

The petals falling as a snowstorm,
the spring is ablaze for weeks
with blossom.
Japan's national flower.

The Sakura Matsuri Festival takes place every spring, usually April, in Japan.

The May Queen

May Day, May Day,
a celebration, an ancient custom.
Spring festival, joyful dancing
around the maypole.
Bells brilliantly belling
Bouncing on ankles,
young persons processing
through their village,
to the May Queen Crowning
in honour of Flora.*

May Day is here.
Bouncing, bowing, bending
beneath the turning maypole,
like an amazing jigsaw coming together.
The children move frolicking,
wearing flowers, singing.
They alone know the true meaning of May Day.

* Flora, Roman goddess of flowers

Lanterns in a Breeze

I wonder why Nature is stirring up our world.
Floods in Australia, cyclones and bushfires.
Earthquakes in Christchurch, and now,
almost too recently, the Pacific ring has fired
again. The end of Time?
Nature, almighty in its wonder,
is in devastation, ground shaking,
buildings swaying like lanterns in a breeze.
overshadowed by nuclear indiscriminations.
Warnings often ignored.

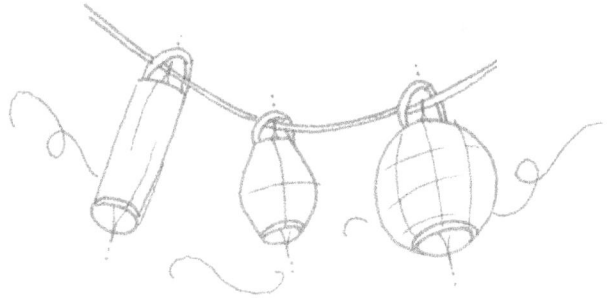

I grieve for Japan, its fine culture, centuries old,
reduced to a nothingness
we cannot imagine or understand.
Even pagan shrines and monuments gone.
People in villages reduced to numbers
too small to be in existence or recovered.

Geisha girls in resplendent kimonos,
beautiful cherry blossom trees,
fountains playing in parks,
religious stones dishevelled,
gone in a dash,
toppled by those roof-high tsunami waves.

Where are those cities, towns, villages.
and *torii* gates keeping watch,
vanished beneath those rushing waters?
Like the 'submerged cathedral'
will they rise again?

The universe in its own Time
will make reparation.
Lost souls will be found,
will create a new future.
Those who perished will not be forgotten.
Rest in peace.

Monet's Garden at Giverny

Come with me into Monet's garden,
the place where he wanted to be,
like those Nymphéas, lilies in his lake,
a lake scintillating with reflections.

Water ponds, a perfect mirror,
announce their presence with glancing light.
White crystal-like shades of water,
bordered with weeping willows
reflecting beside moving lines of evergreen bamboos.
Water lily pads, floating carpets, display
artistic colours familiar in his paintings.

Capturing the aura of a Japanese inspired garden,
the bridge, in green, stands above
its white and pink water bowl
touched on edges with blue, white, yellow and red,
like a light foam of little dots of colour,
yellow and orange points of light.

Beside the garden, a green and pink shuttered house
overlooks a blaze of colour,
red and white geraniums standing proud,
a mass of heads so common,
yet so impressive and beautiful.

Avenues of lavender, peonies and wisteria;
dahlias – nodding purple pinheads,
cobalt blue, magenta, and dark pink –
like sentinels in each row. Poppies, roses,
blue lupins bloom under an azure sky;
bright yellow daisies are hidden away
amidst russet coloured leaves.

It is a painter's garden, his flowers
purple, red and blue, redolent of his artist's palette,
resplendent in the sunlight,
recreate an illusion of brushstrokes on canvas.
Monet's vision, a prism of colour,
a kaleidoscope. Unforgettable.

Painting Light

Colours of Impressionism
resulted in sparkling scenes,
new approaches, novel ideas
in colour and techniques.

Blue shadows evoke mood and atmosphere
with rose and violet hues,
morning mists, the pink of dusk.

Fleeting pictures of light,
gradations of colour captured
on a reflective blanket of white snow,
a landscape's delicate nature in paint.

Monet's sunrise inspires
luminous pure colours with subtle contrasts,
ephemeral visions of light.

Scenes on the banks of the Seine,
stark images of intense light,
scenery rich in nuances of green
reflect colour of Japanese woodblock prints.

The Impressionist's palette
conveys the effects of light,
vivid, versatile and vital colours
awakening a sense of memory
or melancholy.

Colours of Impressionism, Masterpieces from the Musée D'Orsay

Stitched in Memories

My Treasures

My treasures are measures
of my loves and aspirations,
daydreams and fantasies,
fond memories of times past.

A gold necklace lies resplendent,
a charm in its box, rarely worn,
it is treasured with other valuable objects.

I have twenty-five turtles residing in my room.
One is alive, floating in his tank.
Others are small, large, speckled,
jewel-encrusted, not real but splendid.

The real treasures are my books.
Hundreds remind me of the past.
My most cherished are my loves
now a mature memory to last.

Opera, music, British history,
anything English for me a treasure.
A nurtured love, from childhood to university,
precious as they all endure.

They are a lifelong story
of occasions and collections,
my rich journey through time.
Real treasures; intangible,
secure in my memory.

Collections

I wonder why people don't collect
things any more – old-time collections –
how boring.
Not in my house.

My eyes wander round spoons hanging in boxes on walls,
books wall to wall, stamp books hidden in dusty cupboards.
Searched everywhere for books, in country shops,
secondhand, op shops, city bookshops,
overseas shops in little rural villages.

Used to collect stamps, shells, spoons,
popular Monet postcards,
packed in purple photo packets,
meticulously sorted, like a child with a passion.

Now collect assorted bookmarks.
Compulsion. Like a magpie or bowerbird:
must collect all things
pack them away in boxes.

Collections make you observant, curious, particular,
possessive of treasures, gathered, gleaned,
heaped and hoarded in customary stockpiles.
Collections make you buy.
Love them, hate them,
useless,
except to admirers.

Bookmarks

Fun, collecting bookmarks.
Remind me of books, my love of reading.
Oh that I could still read books!
Rely now on other people's reading.

Many categories of bookmark,
indicating style and types.
Unusual ones, overseas, from places I've visited.
Japanese ones decorative. New Zealand, Europe,
Israel, China, and Singapore.

Best the English bookmarks
from all my favourite places,
Scotland and Wales, English history ones,
gifts, like scores of souvenirs,
my own fond purchases.

Bookmarks with Bible texts.
From my book club, the Abbey Girls.
with daffodils, as Daffodil Queen.
Few from Australian places;
interesting Girl Guides,
floral and other categories.

Each section classified with a distinct title.
Over three hundred now in two folders.
Will I ever cease collecting or
enjoying this hobby?

Gifts From Abroad

Epic journey, parents
brought home exotic
reminiscences of new places explored.

Bookmarks from Ireland,
Trinity College, famous in Dublin,
showing photos of gospel books,

illuminated manuscripts in Latin
from the abbey of Kells, St Columba,
hand-scribed 1200 years ago.

Two stunning, splendid shawls,
purple pink patterned
with blue tassels.

The other in greens and blues
of the land, lakes and sky
of the Emerald Isle.

The soul of Russia.
A matryoshka, nesting doll,
hand-painted, national handicraft.

Tartan Tammie hat from bonnie Scotland,
flattering, fashionable, with flair
eye-catching tartan bowties.

Favourite gifts, a dream come true,
a meaningful offering.
Thankful for treasured memories.

For Sale

We first saw the sign FOR SALE
long ago on the fence.
It stayed there for some months,
combined with its neighbour,
octogenarian twins.

Disbelief! Forty-five years
after I last visited.
We'd grieved for it, we missed it.
But it had to go as we moved on.

Would someone want it now?
To love it, cherish it?
Then the sign disappeared.
No one wanted to buy it with its partner.
The house was silent over those summer months,
too hot for anything.

Then, an AUCTION board slipped in by the gate.
New anticipation – someone would respond.
The great day came and went.
No one came to look. What now?
An art deco house no one wants to love and have.
We cared: it had been our home for so long.

Shawls

Today I wore two shawls:
the second one kept the first one warm.
It set me thinking.
Shawls are exotic, trendy,
vibrant in colour, from extraordinary places
both at home and abroad.

Rich colours, intricate designs from
Cambodia, India, Malaysia,
Philippines, Hungary and Germany,
princely purple, magnificent magenta.

Like Persian rugs,
sleek, shiny, shantung
with a hint of silver
amidst the blue sheen.

Long scarves like German shawls,
maybe Austria. Scarves silky, serene,
comforting, upmarket, fashionable,
multi-striped, warm colours.
Shawls streamline, stand alone,
distinguish me,
delicate and delightful.

Some cultures wear shawls every day
I wear shawls on Sunday,
and every day when I am walking out
in winter's cold wind.

Patchwork Quilt

What stories it could tell!
My angel quilt lies cherished
on a good bed in my home.
It came to me by chance,
as if angels had flown in rescuing
it from an undetermined fate.

Pieces of cloth cut exactly, stitched with precision;
purple, patterned, patchwork, plum-coloured,
pink and crimson flowers,
designed by my angels.

A comforter of joy to keep me warm.
Love is embroidered with threads of gold
in all the seams, linking
smooth satin, silk and shiny shantung.
Flowers ornately outlined
in silver beading, each one unique.

Stitched in are the memories
of someone unknown, an angel:
their baby's dress, child's pinafore,
mother's evening dress, a Sunday tablecloth,
long-forgotten floral remnants.

My quilt, a coverlet, is stitched
with love, care, and skilled art,
by angels – 'Log Cabin Angels'
they call themselves,
all bound together in love.

Blood Tests

Blood, veins,
needles, bottles,
readings for all things.

No veins –
despair!
Nurses flinch;
doctors: 'squibs',
call IMVS.

We're here now.
Drop all.
Collecting blood,
a breeze for them.

Not more tests!
I've just had some.
They perform
like Dracula.
Why do they want so much?

Tests are fine,
nil problems.
Next day,
they'll be back.

We love Airlie's blood.
We must collect
more and more and more
to see if the readings are fine.

Now I'm home,
blood is pure,
I'm out of their clutches.

Who's their next victim?
It's not me!

Music

Music is the Beat

Music, the beat of my existence,
the rhythm of my being,
a melody of my life
in harmony with my soul.
Music, loved with all my heart,
shows feelings,
moods, wishes, desires.
We will make music whenever we can.

My masterful memory of masterpieces,
composers of a previous age,
Pachelbel, Bach,
Verdi, Mozart,
Beethoven, Mahler,
many fine composers
for the people of the day.

Modern ones,
Elgar, Britten,
even the Beatles,
gave us music,
made for listening,
making us aware
of the beauty of sound.

MUSIC,
the word which makes
my heart beat with joy.

To Music

Music stirs my soul,
uplifts a mournful mood,
expresses feelings
of the innermost being,
compassion, thought,
the rhythm of life.

Music leads me
down life's path,
roads full of meaning,
people, places.

Music interprets:
moods, desires created
by a passing glimpse of life
in all its modes.

Music inspires:
a ruffled spirit soothed,
a frayed temper mellowed.
A heart rejoices, is happy.

Music makes me happy.
I am keen to hear music
at any time.
Praise God with music.
Sing songs in exultation
for His gift to us.

Music above all is
an epitome of Life.
In passing generations
of styles, genres, sounds,
masterful performances.
Music will live in me forever.

The Opera House

The opera house is mighty
in ambience.
Majestic ceilings,
gold leaf, chandeliers,
elegant pillars supporting
numerous ornate galleries.

The chorus waits in the wings.
The orchestra tunes to the oboe,
the master of wind, and the
violins are poised, hushed
by the imminent arrival of their leader.

Success starts backstage.
Timing is everything:
sets workable, props at hand,
scenery and complex lighting,
costumes donned by soloists,
lined up backstage, awaiting cues.

Sighting special stars,
Sutherland, Bonynge,
Sills and Pavarotti,
temperamental Callas,
Domingo and many others.

The performance begins.
With eager ears and eyes
we consume with passion
the tragedy of *La Bohème*,
the fiery temperament of Lucia,
the comedy of *The Magic Flute*.
I recall a back stage meeting with Domingo
in Covent Garden, London.
The crush of the crowd beckoning
for his pen on my program.
Success! and it started backstage.

The opera house is my home.
Time spent in the company of the masters
produces feelings and emotions
but its real world is behind scenes.

My Destiny

It is an enigma,
a mystery, a curiosity.
My mind cannot escape my feelings.
Locked away in two persons
is my destiny.

I tried so hard.
All consuming,
paper and pen
disseminated my thesis
for what seemed an eternity.

My mind is all-consumed
with nothing else.
Will I be successful?
May I hope to win
this passion for my life?

Graduation Day 2.08.05

My dream is real.
The day has come
to give me honour
and success.

It was a dream of long ago,
impossible at first.
No way, they said,
but, defying the odds
I trod a steady path forward.

Admittedly it took much longer
than for those who walk on feet,
while I, who walk on wheels,
rolled slowly on.

Hard work, much reading,
more writing, but I did not
give up.
Now the time draws near.
What honours will I get?

I have proved my critics wrong.
I have succeeded
with the help of my right hand,
my mother, who stood by me
and encouraged from behind.

Resplendent in cap and gown,
hood, bright green and black.
I will not forget this day.
Honours Musicology:
my heart's desire.

Master of Music

Words are not enough.
Aural appreciation,
intense listening with an ear on edge,
acutely, purposely,
I play the melody in my mind.

Sounds pitched accurately
determine the outcome.
Opera stars, divas
the bathroom tenor
must all strive for perfection.

They are the masters,
of style, of pitch, of timbre, of genre,
not the mere observer
who analyses their performances.

A mere mortal becomes a master
by masterful words,
but the true master is the one
who engages the world.

The Concert Hall

Resounding acoustics,
majestic ceilings,
the concert hall mighty
in ambience.
Gold leaf,
chandeliers,
pillars elegant.

The grand piano stands
resplendent on stage.
The orchestra awaits its leader,
tuning to the magnificent
sound of the oboe,
the master of wind.

The audience awaits
the first melodious sound,
like an expectant father.
Violins poised,
hushed by the arrival of the leader.

The program begins.
With eager ears
we consume with passion
the elegance of Mozart,
the splendour of Mahler,
the verve of Prokofiev.

The concert hall is my home.
I love its feelings,
its emotion,
its masterful command of time,
time spent in the company
of the masters.

Mahler in Concert

Mahler's Fifth, the program cites,
a sprawling opus, intricate in design,
vast and intense.

The concert opens.
Mozart in concerto,
intended as Mahler's forerunner,
steals the show.

Dark pulsating sounds,
a prelude, unexpectedly
providing inspiration
and scintillating ambience.

Reviews in awe of the pianist –
distinctive sounds, though gloomy,
multidimensional, yet personal.
Emotional in complexity,
it probes into my inner being.

We pause for rest.
Do they leave the best to last?
But wait!

Majestic, magnificent Mahler
gloomy and funereal;
stormy and turbulent
moulds my impressions;

The brass distinguished and in tune.
The conductor notable
for producing fine playing.

The program inspires a combination
of genres.
But Mahler gets my vote.

Images of Music

Music makes images
of favourite places.
Ambience remembered
of that uplifting concert.

Music everywhere,
under a tree, by the river,
listen to the sounds
tingling in the sun.

Radio plays music
non-stop classics.
Singers well known
heard with eager ears.

The opera performance
significant, unbelievable,
interpretations unique.
Sounds invade all facets of life.

The baby with her rattle.
or a night-time lullaby.
A schoolgirl learning piano,
her first instrument.

The school band plays imaginatively.
Scholars perform the old masters,
as well as new, to everyone.
Music replenishes the whole being.

Bells

Bells ring for many things,
part of our life,
our heritage,
communicate messages.

Foretell of doom,
imminent danger.
Rejoice with all.
What do they say?

Fire bells, church bells,
calls to worship,
dinner bells.
Lost without them?

Muffled bells,
drone bells,
glockenspiels,
carillons, school bells.
What do they tell us?

Concert bells,
interval is over.
Bells on animals,
cats and cows.
Will we find them?

Cathedral bells
peal out on Christmas Day,
joyous with all people
at the Saviour's birth.

A bell at Bethlehem?
No! A star tells us
the way we should go.

My Heart Rejoices

When music is played,
my heart rejoices.
Music calms at all times.
Rejoice and be happy.

Music enlivens the day.
When I hear Bach,
I feel enlightened.
Mozart gives me feelings of refinement.

Beethoven stirs the passions within me,
Mahler makes me passionate and strong.
Elgar rouses feelings
of England, my heritage,
of my great love for this fine land.

Britten is my favourite composer, of modern times.
He brings great lyrical beauty to music
and a diversity of harmonies
which enrich my soul.

Music is above all an epitome of life
in passing generations;
of styles, genres, of sounds,
and masterful performances.
Music will live with me forever.

Hopes and Aspirations

A Kaleidoscope of Dreams

Life is full of hope,
ideas abound
related to inspiration,
longing to succeed.
Abstract ideas help lateral thinking.

I dream of visits to England,
to my favourite places.
Dreams and ambitions for today –
tomorrow never comes.

Living in my dreams
will I realise my hopes –
of visits to unknown places,
to a concert or opera,
new clothes every day?

Will I need more dreams
to urge me on?
Bringing the outside world in –
dreams of peace, no more war –
capturing every essence
    of the dream in reality.
Real things pervade my mind.
Books unread,
success with my poetry book.
I strive forward, do not look back,
taking every opportunity.

Dreams, thoughts, ideas come to me
in the darkness of the night:
every dream is cherished,
comprehended, finding depth
in all my memories.

Hope

We need hope
ever before us.
Hope spurs us on.
It is our strength.

Enduring passions
are created by hope.
We live for our dreams,
our aspirations.

Without hope we are lost,
homeless without direction.
Hope is our compass,
our direction finder.
Hope for quality in our life.

New Year

Hopes, resolutions.
I stand back and think:
Hope is helpful
Overwhelming,
Pure,
Everlasting.

Realising my efforts is an exciting prospect.
But why do we need resolutions?
Are we blind to our whims and failure?
The New Year rings in again,
unfailing, arrives amidst
a flurry of fierce fireworks.

Eyes all look skyward.
The world lights up for a
fresh New Year.
Does this exhilarating beginning
imbue a spirit of hope?

At last the past year has gone, forever.
A new era, a chance to do better?
To have greater hopes for mankind?

Time will tell – already forgotten
are the defects of the old year?
Let us rejoice, and be glad.
Our time is in our own hands.

What Love Means

Love is unlimited in my home.
We all love one another.
with infinitesimal depth.

Love is not masterful
unless it is coupled with a family
who are one with each other.
Members of my family
are loving and kind.
They thrive on love.

Love which knows no bounds
is a mode for anyone
who is loving.
We are loving when we know God.
Love is from Him. It abides forever.

We must make the best of a situation.
Love holds us together:
like a chain mesh in a jewellery piece.
Love is timeless, like the universe
showing all its majesty.

We thrive on love in our family.
We achieve all things through our love
interwoven in all we do and say.
We are masterful always in our family love.

2000 and Beyond

'2000'
Enthralling, exciting.
Looks forward, develops, creates.
A new era begins.
Millennium.

Hopeful, expectant.
Anticipates, cherishes, indulges.
We have faith in tomorrow.
Futurity.

'And beyond.'
Unimaginable, unknown.
Ordained, foreshadowed, determined.
My mind cannot comprehend.
Tomorrow.

Doubtful, insecure.
Frightens, brightens, inspires.
We move with the tide of time.
Destiny.

My Dream

My book will be launched,
not like a ship
with champagne,
but with an eye-catching cover
depicting the light
I have found.

My dream is not only light but reality.
Look forward to the day
when all will be revealed:
my innermost thoughts,
my journey, of love, of endurance,
my inspirations.

I've reached the light,
my goal, my dream
of telling everyone my story.
Stunning, enlightening, whimsical,
challenging impressions.
This milestone is a reward
of my faith in God.

Ownership

It has taken a long time
to see my new journal article on line.
a masterful effort on my part.

My writing leaves my house by a cable.
Flies round the world
by means of a web.
Last week, six people in the States and Canada
read my thesis floating there online,
Astounding!

My article will join it there soon,
ready to jump on the web
like an athletic spider.
My sound tracks need to have
copyright permission before they can go too.
Who is the owner? Am I?
Or are there several?

Today, owners are invisible.
Letters ignored, unanswered.
Emails sent, no replies.
messages sit in voice mail
or inboxes, unheard,
Frustrating!

We struck the jackpot, this morning.
Someone was waiting for our call.
My article is now poised, permission granted,
ready to be uploaded,
about to reach out to the world.
Will anyone read it?

It is shared with the world,
its new pseudo-owner,
like Facebook,
but more stylish, scholarly,
and satisfying to every opera buff.

Peace

For everything there is a season;
a time for war, a time for peace.
But must there be more time
for war than peace?

Man's greed knows no bounds;
it multiplies more and more.
Man aspires to that which is not his.
And then there is war.

Man persists in his own destruction;
battles and fighting never cease.
When will man open his eyes
to the beauty of peace?

Peace shines apart,
waiting to be accepted by man.
But as so few seek eternal peace,
how long can earthly unity last?

I, too, have searched for peace;
It seemed an unattainable goal.
until a still small voice spoke

from deep within my soul.
The quality of peace is not strained;
It droppeth as the gentle rain from heaven
upon the heated war…

Promises

Promises – gilded, moral, upright, meaningful.
Always unbroken? Create trust.
Doing one's best encourages achievement.
Others do not always have that mission.

Promises – broken, slightly or smashed,
silvery not gold.
Unwritten words, let downs,
unfulfilled actions

intent on their own purposes.
Those who break promises
fall deeply, create unhappiness,
loss of faith in human beings.

Promises are for keeps.
Infused with faith and trust,
a rainbow in the sky is *the* promise.
God's promises are never broken.

Musings

Poetry, my love.
Words I read from Isaiah
stimulate my thoughts –
'Let me sing for my beloved
a love song.'[1]

Isaiah, a master of vocabulary.
How is it that poetic thought
from words so long ago,
reaches out to me –
prophetic, encouraging,
wise and thought-provoking?

Down the ages
poetry has soothed mankind,
kept him strong, emotional
compassionate.

Medieval Chaucer pens romance,
earthy and miraculous tales.
Shakespeare indicts history,
proverbial sayings,
well-spoken quotations.

Coleridge bestows a meditative mind,
Wordsworth calls up memories,
sensuous nostalgia,
emotions recollected in tranquillity,
warming hues and seasons of happiness.
Keats finds melancholy in delight,
a dream world.

Pushkin strides there;
to where shows a free mind,
lyrical, satirical, intuitive and realist:
hides the depth of his soul in poetry.

Wilfred Owen evokes
the depth and pity of war
Auden, unsentimental
but thoughtful imagery –
a poet of his time.

Modern poetry, with
expressions of deep feeling
has desires, whims, fancies.

Turn to poetry any time.
It calms my being,
an escape to new worlds,
new horizons.
The words of Isaiah ring again in my mind:
'Be glad and rejoice
for ever in that which I create.'[2]

Poetry stirs my soul.
I care only for my love,
my language of motivation and spirit,
my song of joy,
my love song.

1. Isaiah 5:1
2. Isaiah 68:17

Friendly Books

My books are my friends,
separate beings, companions, teachers, comforters.
Found many friends while scrounging
in dusty old second-hand bookshops.
Many well born from preloved owners of long ago.

Like shining stars in the sky,
they are found in libraries,
cupboards built in parks
where books are brought and exchanged.
Amassed on all my shelves are my friends.

I long to read them all again.
What anecdotes will I find?
What warmth, what memories?
Pleasure will be my outcome.

I cannot read them all now.
I wait for someone to read them to me.
The readers will become my friends.

Stars

Look up at the stars.
A vast universe, like dreams,
hope for the future.
All indistinct, yet so real
like life as a new poet.

My thoughts are like words
flowing through me as lifeblood;
my aspirations, my stars,
mainstreams of reality.
Wish to write poems always.

www.ingramcontent.com/pod-product-compliance
Lightning Source LLC
Chambersburg PA
CBHW070915080526
44589CB00013B/1301